# Mystic Minerals

## Wisdom of the Ancients

By
## Barbara J. Matteson

**COSMIC RESOURCES:**
**Seattle, Washington**

Library of Congress Catalog Card Number 86-71607

Copyright ©COSMIC RESOURCES, 1985.

COSMIC RESOURCES
P.O. Box 913
Langley, Washington 98260
(206) 221-8574

Revised Edition

10    9    8    7    6    5

Typesetting by Dataprose, a Division of Bozotronics, Seattle, WA.

ISBN 0-9620524-O-X

My thanks to Bob for sharing his knowledge about geology.

To all womyn,
  I hope you will accept my usage of the term "man" within this text to include all the womyn of the world.

Barbara Matteson

# Table of Contents

# History

For thousands of years different peoples in different countries around the world have used gemstones for healing. Some groups used rough stones. Other groups used cut stones. And certain groups used nature's organic gems, such as coral, in their natural state.

Some people believed that stones were able to heal by the energy they were said to possess. Other people believed that stones healed by their color. Still others believed that stones had a power to heal only in partnership with specific minerals or metals.

In some cultures healing stones were ground and then ingested. In other cultures it was customary to drink the fluid a healing stone was steeped in. And in many cultures stones were thought to heal only if placed directly on the body.

But not all people used the energy they believed stones possessed for beneficial reasons. Individuals tried to use the power of stones to profit at the expense of others. They used the energy of stones to cast spells and to torment people with the Evil Eye. In response the victims learned to use stones as talismans and amulets to ward off Evil Eye, break spells and protect against negative influences. They learned to use the energy of stones to heal their emotions and psyches as well as their bodies.

Even today there are people throughout the world who believe in the healing properties of Nature's organic and inorganic gemstones. These people believe that there is a universal energy shared by all animate and, seemingly, inanimate objects. Perhaps they are right. After all, isn't it common for people to ingest minerals and vitamins to boost their energy?

Individuals may scoff at such beliefs, assuming that only ignorant people would believe "inanimate" objects have energy. But if these individuals would look around they would see how dependent man is on Nature's gemstones. Rubies are used to amplify light in lasers. Quartz is used in solar cells, watch batteries and LEDs. And of course man is very dependent on the energy inherent in carbon for heat, fuel and plastics.

Regardless of your beliefs about gemstones you must admit that these flowers of the Mineral Kingdom have long fascinated Man. We all can wonder at the symmetry of crystals, the range of their colors and the unusual habitats of specimens. Explore the world of minerals and you might just explore the fascinating world of your self.

# Stones

Stones, both organic and inorganic, have historically been attributed power. The following listing attempts to inform the reader of the most widely held beliefs regarding individual stones. When known, the astrological, ray and chakra associations for each stone is listed within the parentheses directly following the stone's name.

**AGATE** Often used as worry-stones. Calming during times of stress. Come in full range of colors. See Fire-, Iris-, Moss-, and Snakeskin Agate.

**ALEXANDRITE** (Pluto, 7th Chakra) A rare gemstone regarded as having regenerative power. It was said to enhance the re-birth of both the inner and outer self.

**ALMANDINE** (Scorpio, 6th Ray, 1st Chaka) *Heart trouble.* Inspires during times of contemplation. Balances peace and solitude. Represents profound love. Also called Red Garnet.

**AMAZONITE** (Virgo, 5th Chakra) Soothing to the nerves when wearer is bombarded with irritating energy.

**AMBER** (Sun, 5th Ray, 2nd Chakra) *Goiter.* Allows body to heal itself by the amber absorbing negative energy. Sunny color helps to calm the nerves.

**AMETHYST** (Pisces, 7th Ray, 6th Chakra) *Insomnia.* Controls temperament by imparting a soothing and calming influence. Helps business affairs prosper. Used in meditation.

**APACHE TEARS OBSIDIAN** (Saturn, 1st Chakra) Traditionally considered the tears of mourning women for the warriors driven off a cliff by the Cavalry. See also Obsidian.

**APATITE** (Gemini, 3rd Chakra) Stone of the future. Will bring knowledge to those attuned to it by clearing mental confusion. Awakens the finer, inner self.

**AQUAMARINE** (Gemini, 3rd Ray, 5th Chakra) *Swollen glands.* Quickens one's intelligence. Makes one unconquerable through learning about one's self.

**ASTERIA** General term of stones showing asterism, star pattern, when cut in cabachon form; i.e., star ruby, star garnet, star quartz.

**AVENTURINE FELDSPAR** See Sunstone.

**AVENTURINE QUARTZ** (Uranus) *Skin Diseases.* Considered good luck in love matters. Promotes independence and originality.

**AZURITE** (Sagittarius, 6th Chakra) Stimulates visual images during meditation. Develops self-confidence. Helps psychic talents evolve.

**AZURMALACHITE** (5th Chakra) Gives comfort by calming anxious state associated with dis-ease. Allows the thought process to follow its course enabling one to render ineffective emotionally charged thoughts.

**BARITE** (Uranus) Symbolizes the realization that all things are possible. Enhances friendship, harmony and love. Also called Desert Rose.

**BERYL** Family name for Aquamarine, Emerald and Heliodor.

**BLACK CORAL** (Saturn) Said to absorb negativity of the wearer. Imparts tranquility.

**BLACK SAPPHIRE** Used to protect one from all harms. See also Sapphire.

**BLACK TOURMALINE.** See Schorl.

**BLOODSTONE** (Aries, 1st Chakra) *Spleen.* Makes one unselfish and idealistic. Improves talents, enhances creative efforts and helps in decision-making processes. Also called Heliotrope.

**BLUE SAPPHIRE** Used to heal the heart, mind and body. See also Sapphire.

**BLUE SPINEL** (Jupiter) Calms sexual desire. See also Spinel.

**CAIRNGORM** See Smoky Quartz.

**CALCITE** (Moon, 3rd Chakra) Releases electrical impulses when put under pressure. Energy amplifier. See Iceland Spar.

**CARBUNCLE** An Almandine cut in cabachon fashion. See Almandine.

**CARNELIAN** (Taurus, 6th Ray, 2nd Chakra) *Neuralgia*. Protects against envy, fear and rage. Banishes sorrow. See also Pink Carnelian.

**CAT'S EYE** (Gemini) *Bowel cramps*. Said to help during intellectual undertakings. Provides a stabilizing influence thereby strengthening one's resolve. Also called Cymophane.

**CELESTITE** (Gemini, 5th Chakra) Reported to attune one to one's elevated reasoning powers.

**CHALCEDONY** (Moon, 4th Ray) "Mother Stone." Signifies charity. Increases good will, adds vigor and reduces touchiness. It's said to cure forms of lunacy.

**CHIASTOLITE** Historically associated with repelling Evil Eye. Reputed to cure fevers, staunch the flow of the blood, increase the secretion of milk in nursing mothers. Also called Cross Stone.

**CHRYSOBERYL** (Sun, 5th Ray) *Adrenal glands*. Increases generosity. Allows one to forgive family members or friends who may have done an injustice. Brings peace of mind.

**CHRYSOCOLLA** (Gemini, 5th Chakra) *Feminine Discomfort*. Allows peace by easing the pain of anger and sorrow. Advances sensitivity towards others.

**CHRYSOLITE** See Peridot.

**CHRYSOPRASE** (Venus, 4th Chakra) Reduces superiority or inferiority complexes. Makes one adaptable. Imparts fluency of speech, presence of mind.

5

**CINNABAR** See Mercury.

**CITRINE** (Gemini, 5th Ray, 3rd Chakra) *Circulation of blood.* Influences education, business, familial and interpersonal matters. Promotes sunny and cheerful demeanor.

**CLEAR QUARTZ** See Rock Crystal.

**COPPER** (Venus) *Arthritis.* Positively influences the flow of blood within the body. Used to cleanse wounds and fight bacterial infection. Brings luck to person, especially in recovery of property.

**CORAL** See Black-, Pink- and Red Coral.

**COWRIE** (Neptune) *Fertility.* Ancient symbol for creation or birth. Reputedly inspires creativity, gives power, allows artistic fulfillment and promises wealth.

**CROSS STONE** See Chiastolite.

**CYMOPHANE** See Cat's Eye.

**DESERT ROSE** See Barite.

**DIAMOND** (Aries, 1st Ray) *Poisoning.* Talisman against cowardice. Rallies strength in old age. Maintains unity and love. Traditionally the power of the diamond works only when the diamond is freely given.

**DOUBLE TERMINATED QUARTZ CRYSTAL** Used in meditation and astral projection.

**ELBAITE** (Libra, 6th Ray, 4th Chakra) *Falls.* Allows one to trust in the power of love. Gives a joy and enthusiasm for life by releasing destructive feelings. Also called Pink Tourmaline.

**EMERALD** (Taurus, 3rd Ray, 4th Chakra) *Spine.* Enhances memory and mental powers. Quiets emotions.

**FAIRY STONE** See Staurolite.

**FELDSPAR** Family name for Amazonite, Labrodorite, Moonstone and Sunstone.

**FIRE AGATE** (Capricorn, 1st Chakra) Represents the spiritual flame of goodness. It is said to drive away fear, to give protection from all dangers and to banish bad aspirations.

**FLINT** (Pluto) *Kidneystone.* Helps relieve shyness and promotes interpersonal experiences. Talisman for mental and physical strength when fighting enemies. Substance of man's first tools.

**FLOATING STONE** See Pumice.

**FLOURITE** (Neptune, 6th Chakra) "Genius Stone." Increases ability to concentrate. Balances the positive and negative relationships of the mind. Helps one see reality behind illusion.

**GALENA** See Lead.

**GARNET** See Almandine and Uvarovite.

**GOLD** (Sun) *Mental faculties.* Attracts honors, wealth and happiness. Calms one, stabilizes nerves, amplifies positive feelings. Attunes one to nature and its healing forces.

**GOLDEN BERYL** See Heliodor.

**GREEN GARNET** See Uvarovite.

**GREEN TOURMALINE** (Capricorn, 6th Ray, 4th Chakra) *Constipation.* Inspires creativity. Attracts success, prosperity and abundance.

**GYPSUM** "Lucky Stone." Strong influence for bringing good fortune to the owner.

**HELIODOR** (Sun, 7th Chakra) Influences the mental plane. Brings about a balance between the intuitive and conscious levels of the self. Also called Golden Beryl.

**HELIOTROPE** See Bloodstone.

**HEMATITE** (Mars) *Leg Cramps.* Focuses energy and emotions for balance between the mind, body and spirit.

**HYACINTH** See Zircon.

**ICELAND SPAR** (Moon, 3rd Chakra) Optical quality calcite. Property of double-refraction reminds one of double meaning of words.

**INDICOLITE** (Venus) It is said to enhance the emanations of loving and passionate impressions. Represents harmonious ideas. Also called Blue Tourmaline.

**IRIS AGATE** (Jupiter) Awakens the inner self. Makes one receptive to truth. Promotes happiness, longevity, good health and the friendship of others.

**IRON** (Mars) *Blood.* Brings mental and emotional balance. Confers invulnerability. Favorably influences the outcome of lawsuits, petitions and judgments.

**IVORY** (Jupiter) Represents purity. Promotes purpose for rallying strength.

**JACINTH** See Zircon.

**JADE** (Pisces, 3rd Ray) "The Dream Stone." *Bladder trouble.* Attunes one to the needs of others. Inspires wisdom when judging problems. Traditionally represents a long life with a peaceful end.

**JADEITE** Reportedly releases pent-up emotions through the dream process if a piece of jadeite is placed under the pillow before going to sleep.

**JASPER** (Leo, 4th Ray) "The Mother of all stones." *Loss of sense of smell.* Reputed to soothe the nerves and cure a queasy stomach. Also called Silex.

**JET** (Saturn) *Migraine.* Dispells fearful thoughts. Guards against illness or violence to wearer.

**KUNZITE** (Pluto, 7th Ray, 4th Chakra) Represents maturity. Allows one to feel secure, open, strong, loving and vibrant. Clears the mental and emotional aspects of one's self.

**LABRODORITE** (Sagittarius, 6th Chakra) Protects one's aura. Helps keep aura balanced, protected, free from energy leaks.

**LAPIS LAZULI** (Sagittarius, 2nd Ray, 6th Chakra) *Depression.* Brings tranquility, self-confidence and a cheerful frame of mind. Promotes sound sleep. It's said to bring success in love matters.

**LAZULITE** Typically used as a worry stone. Calms one, allows one to sense self-worth.

**LAZURITE** Principal mineral of Lapis lazuli. Promotes tranquility and spiritual quality to wearer.

**LEAD** (Saturn) *Sores.* Said to reduce inflammations, heal pimples, reduce ulcers on the body. Stops unhealthy lusting. Also called Galena.

**LODESTONE** See Magnetite.

**MAGNETITE** (Mercury, 1st Ray) *Nose bleed.* This is a stone of stability. It is used to attract love. Enables one to project mind, view things from a distance. Also called Lodestone.

**MALACHITE** (Saturn, 3rd Ray, 4th Chakra) *Asthma.* Helps one rule wisely by subconscious understanding. Represents fidelity in love and friendship.

**MALACHITE & AZURITE** See Azurmalachite.

**MARCASITE** Represents spiritual development. Shows how one may appear dull to others but is actually bright if one will allow real self to shine.

**MERCURY** (Mercury) *Weight.* Imparts elegant and fluid movement. Brings gift of eloquence. Aids merchants in acquiring wealth. Also called Cinnabar and Quicksilver.

**METEORITE** Considered a gift from other worlds. Similar to Tektite but of a metallic nature. See Tektite.

**MOONSTONE** (Cancer, 4th Chakra) *Pulmonary consumption.* Talisman of good fortune. It keeps that which is dear to one closer. It is said to arouse tender passions and bring happiness.

**MOSS AGATE** (Cancer) Makes one agreeable and persausive, strong and victorious. Improves ego and self-esteem. Promotes the growth of crops. It's said to help one acquire riches.

**NEPHRITE** (Libra) *Renal colic.* Used as a talisman by the Maoris of New Zealand. Used in weapons, tools and jewelry by the Ancients.

**OBSIDIAN** (Saturn) Reflects one's flaws and shows what changes are needed. Focuses internal vision. See also Apache Tears Obsidian.

**OLIVINE** See Peridot.

**ONYX** (Leo, 1st Chakra) *Bone marrow.* Banishes grief. Enhances self-control, especially to make wise decisions. Encourages happiness and good fortune.

**OPAL** (Cancer, 4th Chakra) *Eyesight.* Amplifies one's traits thereby giving confidence to overcome poor qualities. Enhances memory. Represents faithful love.

**PADPARADSCHAH SAPPHIRE** (Libra) Brings knowledge of human nature to wearer. Enhances ability to understand others' intentions. Makes one cheerful and friendly. Commonly referred to as "Pad."

**PEARL** (Moon) *Digestion.* Signifies Faith, Charity and Innocence. Embellishes personal integrity. Helps one focus one's attention.

**PERIDOT** (Virgo, 3rd Ray, 4th Chakra) Acts as tonic to system to strengthen and regenerate the body. Helps heal bruised egos by lessening anger or jealousy. Also called Chrysolite and Olivine.

**PINK CARNELIAN** Encourages love between parents and children. See also Carnelian.

**PINK CORAL** (Cancer) Represents continuity, activity and form as seen in the building of coral colonies.

**PINK TOURMALINE** See Elbaite.

**PLATINUM** *Pineal gland.* Keeps one animated in order to accomplish goals. Fights chronic constipation.

**PUMICE** (Jupiter) Awed people by being able to float on water although made of stone. Reminds one to not sink into despair when faced by weighty problems. Also called Floating Stone.

**PYRITE** (Sun) *Bronchitis.* Symbolizes the warmth and lasting presence of the sun. Recalls the beautiful memories of friendship and love.

**QUARTZ** See Aventurine Quartz, Double Terminated Quartz Crystal, Rock Crystal and Rutilated Quartz.

**QUICKSILVER** See Mercury.

**RED CORAL** (Venus, 6th Ray) *Colic.* Attunes one to nature. Connects one with creative forces and wisdom. It's said to protect one against melancholy.

**RED GARNET** See Almandine.

**RED SPINEL** (Scorpio) Makes one strong and tough for all encounters. See also Spinel.

**RED TOURMALINE** See Rubellite.

**RHODOCHROSITE** (Pluto) Removes tendency towards avoidance or denial. Makes one accepting, willing to integrate or assimilate new information.

**RHODONITE** (6th Ray, 1st Chakra) *Emphysema.* Helps one achieve greatest potential. Dispels anxiety. Makes one coherent.

**ROCK CRYSTAL** (Aquarius, 1st Ray, 7th Chakra) *Vertigo.* Promotes patience and perseverance. Provides restful sleep. Used extensively in meditation and spiritual development. Also called Clear Quartz.

**ROSE QUARTZ** (Venus, 4th Chakra) *Vertigo.* Makes one receptive to the beauty of art, music and the written word. Enlivens one's imagination. Represents a younger and warmer love, though not so lasting.

**RUBELLITE** (Scorpio, 6th Ray) Strengthens the will to sacrifice in the name of love. Intensifies and directs devotional urges. Also called Red Tourmaline.

**RUBY** (Leo, 6th Ray, 2nd Chakra) *Fever.* Gathers and amplifies energy, helping mental concentration. Enhances success in controversies, disputes or war. Brings knowledge, health, wealth and spiritual wisdom.

**RUTILE** (Gemini) *Bronchitis* Used for healing and balancing the aura by repelling negative energy.

**RUTILATED QUARTZ** Rutile is an inclusion which is said to intensify the power of quartz crystals.

**SAPPHIRE** (Virgo, 2nd Ray, 6th Chakra) *Hemorrhage.* Chases away evil thoughts. Brings joy and peace of mind. Opens mind to beauty and intuition. See also Black-, Blue-, Padparadschah-, Star-, and White Sapphire.

**SARD** (Aries) Historically used as protectant against sorcery and incantations. It is said to render the wearer fearless and victorious.

**SARDONYX** (Mars, 3rd Ray) Brings happiness in marriage, delight in living. Attracts friends and good fortune. Encourages self-control.

**SCHORL** (Capricorn) Repels negativity and the possibility of being victimized by others' negative energies. Keeps one's light shining even in darkest hour.

**SELENITE** (Taurus, 7th Chakra) Gives clarity of mind. Expands awareness of self and surroundings.

**SERPENTINE** (Cancer, 4th Ray) Historically was used to

draw out poison from the body if one is bitten by a venomous creature.

**SILEX** See Jasper.

**SILVER** (Moon) *Hepatitis.* Improves quality of speech. Helps cleanse the body's system through its pores. Brings great advantage throughout life.

**SMOKY QUARTZ** (Capricorn, 1st Chakra) *Anus.* Activates survival instincts. Improves intuition regarding challenges and responsibilities. Brings personal pride and joy in living. Used in meditation. Also called Cairngorm.

**SNAKESKIN AGATE** (Leo, 4th Ray) *Hearing problems.* Promotes pleasing personality through inner peace, joy of life and good cheer to all. Gives strength during times of much activity.

**SODALITE** (Sagittarius, 2nd Ray, 6th Chakra) *Gland metabolism.* Gives one the ability to think rationally and come to logical conclusions.

**SPINEL** Renews energy allowing one to make another attempt at difficult tasks. See also Blue- and Red Spinel.

**STAR SAPPHIRE** Used to help center thoughts. See also Sapphire.

**STAUROLITE** Talisman of good luck. Reputed to be the crystalized tears of fairies. Also called Fairy Stone.

**SUGILITE** (Pisces, 6th Chakra) *Dis-ease.* Brings realization of connection between well-being of the body and the mind. Attracts healing power.

**SULPHUR** (Leo, 3rd Chakra) *Thrush.* Enhances physical radiance.

**SUNSTONE** (Libra, 4th Chakra) Makes one independent and original. Brings luck in games. Also called Aventurine Feldspar.

**TEKTITE** Encourages one to gather knowledge throughout life's travels. Hinders scarring of the heart due to bad experiences. Similar to Meteorites but principally vitreous.

**TIGER EYE** (Saturn, 4th Ray) *Eye Disease.* Makes one aware of the needs of the self and of others. Its pulsating image gives out soothing and settling vibrations.

**TIN** (Jupiter) *Chest.* Clears lungs of consumption. Heals sores and ulcers. Kills intestinal worms.

**TSAVORITE** See Uvarovite.

**TOPAZ** (Sagittarius, 5th Ray, 3rd Chakra) *Loss of sense of taste.* Brings out individuality and creative power. Encourages confidence in trusting one's decisions. Replaces negativity with love and joy.

**TORTOISE SHELL** (Mercury) Embodies the fight between Light and Dark in its translucent beauty. Represents the exchange of male and female qualities.

**TOURMALINE** *Intestinal tract.* Attracts inspiration, dispels fear, bestows self-confidence. See also Elbaite, Green Tourmaline, Indicolite, Rubellite, Schorl and Watermelon Tourmaline.

**TURQUOISE** (Capricorn, 2nd Ray, 5th Chakra) *Headache.* Induces wisdom and understanding. Influences trust, kindness and acknowledgment of beauty. Reputedly influences a spontaneous upsurge of romantic love.

**UVAROVITE** (Aquarius) *Sexual hormones.* Bestows solitude, peace and quiet without making one lonely. Helps clear thoughts. Also called Green Garnet and Tsavorite.

**WATERMELON TOURMALINE** (Scorpio, 4th Ray, 4th Chakra) *Nervousness.* Allows serious people to see the humor in experiences. Lightens one's emotional load allowing nature's beauty to be experienced.

**WHITE SAPPHIRE** Used to focus attention when mind is confused. See also Sapphire.

**ZIRCON** (Aries, 1st Ray) *Allergies.* Helps one overcome sadness and suspicion. Enhances one's independence and self-confidence. Also called Hyacinth and Jacinth.

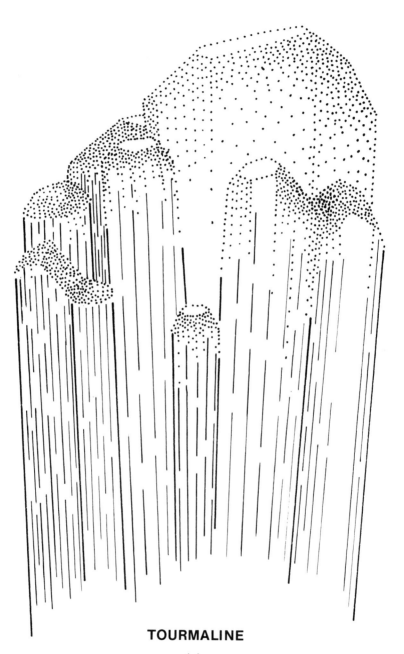

**TOURMALINE**

14

# Personalizing Your Stones

People come into possession of stones and crystals in a variety of ways. A person may happen upon a stone while out for a walk. A person may deliberately go "hunting" for a stone in one of the unlimited number of rock-hounding locations. A person may purchase a stone or crystal for his or her personal enjoyment. When purchasing a stone, choose one that attracts you, but that doesn't mean it has to be attractive. The stone that draws you to it may be imperfect, blemished and absolutely unattractive to someone else. You might want to take the stone in hand to see if it is as comfortable for you to hold as to gaze upon.

Once you have acquired a crystal or stone, it is common practice to cleanse and then program it for your use. Traditionally, stones given to one out of love do not need to be cleansed, only programmed. But crystals or stones acquired in other manners are usually cleansed before programming. The cleansing is performed in order to expell any negative energy the stone may have accumulated before coming into your life.

Some materials that stones are immersed in for cleansing are: sand, cedar chips, wood ash, denatured alcohol, spring water and sea water. If sea water is not readily available you can make it from sea salt and bottled water, both of which are found in health food stores. Keep the

15

stones and crystals immersed and in a dark place, such as a closet, for at least 24 hours. Remove your stones from the cleansing material and then expose them to either sunlight or moonlight for a total of 24 hours. Now you are ready to program your stones. You may program them for their historically associated qualities or for the qualities you want in your own life. Hold one of the stones in your hand. Relax. Concentrate on the quality you want associated with your personal stone. When the association between the stone and the quality has been made, you'll feel comfort surround you. Each of your crystals and stones should be programmed in this manner.

If you wish to share your stones with others, do so. But you should avoid having people touch any of your stones without permission. The negativity or skepticism of people can be transferred. You will then need to cleanse and program your stones again.

# Storage of Stones

Perhaps in a childhood Science class your teacher taught you about static electricity. One of the popular classroom demonstrations for creating static electricity was to rub silk on a glass rod. The silk took on a positive charge. And the glass took on a negative charge.

Many people these days are carrying their quartz crystals and related stones in silk pouches. Quartz, also called silicon dioxide, is the major component of glass. Now, consider what the friction of carrying your quartz-based stones in a silk container does to the charge of your crystals.

Other popular containers for stones are pouches made of rayon velvet or brocade. Admittedly, the pouches have an aesthetic appeal. But synthetics also can create static electricity when rubbed against quartz-based stones. Why would anyone endanger the energy charge of crystals after taking the time to cleanse and then program their personal crystals?

Historically, sacred stones were wrapped in animal skins. Some people these days consider keeping stones in leather archaic or even barbaric. But these same people consider the information which these "barbaric" cultures have handed down to us about crystals as being the final word on crystals' powers.

As stated before, leather pouches were used to house the sacred stones of various cultures throughout millenium. Anthropologists worldwide continue to find crystals and stones contained in animal skin, although the exact reasoning for leather is unknown. Today, leather is used as a cushioning, insulating and grounding material for crystals. Leather, too, has an aesthetic appeal due to its scent, texture and appearance. And more importantly, animal skin does not create static electricity when rubbed against quartz-based stones.

# The Power
# of Engraved Stones

Engraving stones with symbols, lettering or figures has been common since pre-history. Most of the reasoning behind engraving a stone has been lost to modern man. But some reasons, both selfish and unselfish, have survived throughout time. Those reasons are listed below.

**Agate** engraved with a dog's head and a lion was used to protect one from epilepsy and plague.

**Amethyst** engraved with a bear and put in a silver setting was used to prevent drunkenness. When Amethyst was engraved with the sun and the moon, it was used to ward off incantations, evil influences or secret plot of sorcerers.

**Beryl** of sea green color when engraved with a frog and set in gold gains for the owner the affection of anyone who touches or is touched by it.

**Bloodstone** engraved with a bat gave the wearer power over demons.

**Carnelian** engraved with the image of a man holding a sceptre in his hand was used to stop hemorrhages and also to bring good luck.

**Chalcedony** when white of color and engraved with a man riding horseback at full speed and brandishing a pike in his right hand was used to protect the traveler. When Chalcedony is engraved with a man with his right hand aloft it ensures success in lawsuits.

**Emerald** engraved with the image of a starling was supposed to strengthen eyes.

**Garnet** when engraved with a lion was used to preserve good health.

**Jasper** engraved with a cross kept one from drowning. When Jasper was engraved with a kite tearing apart a serpent it helped women during pregnancy.

**Lodestone** engraved with a man in armor made the wearer victorious in war.

**Moonstone** engraved with a swallow brought the wearer the good-will and friendship of all.

**Onyx** engraved with the head of Andromeda produced terrifying dreams to those who wore it.

**Peridot** engraved with the figure of an ass protected one from gout. If engraved with a vulture it protected the wearer against wind storms.

**Red Coral** engraved with a man bearing a sword protected one from epidemics.

**Ruby** engraved with a dragon made the wearer joyous and healthy.

**Sapphire** engraved with a ram was used to cure eye inflammations, bring good luck, preserve chastity. Engraved with an astrolabe the sapphire enabled the wearer to predict the future.

**Sard** engraved with intertwining ivy and grape vines was the stone of good fortune for women.

**Sardonyx** engraved with an eagle and set in gold was a bringer of good luck.

**Topaz** engraved with a falcon was used to acquire the good-will of people in powerful positions.

When a stone is engraved with the sign of its corresponding zodiacal influence it is said to maximize the power of the stone.

# The Wearing of Stones

Man has seemingly always enjoyed the ceremonial aspects of life. Daily rites, such as the "proper" wearing of a stone gave pleasure to many. The correct manner in which a stone was worn was said to enhance the stone's power. Even today there are people who wear stones in only prescribed fashion.

Below are some of the ways that stones were to be worn on the person.

**Amber** should be worn on the throat as a pendant or necklace.

**Azurite** should be worn against the skin. Some suggest setting azurite in a ring and wearing it on the right hand. Others suggest wearing it on the center of the forehead.

**Aquamarine** should be worn as a pendant or necklace over the thymus.

**Chrysoberyl** should be placed in the navel or over the solar plexus.

**Citrine** should be set in gold in a manner so that when it is worn the termination of the citrine crystal faces downward.

**Copper** should be worn in bracelet form on either wrist.

**Coral** should be worn against the flesh, usually about the neck.

**Diamonds** are best worn in conjunction with other stones, such as emerald and amethyst. Roman warriors wore a diamond talisman on their left arm.

**Garnet** should be worn over the Third Eye.

**Gold** can be worn in combination with other minerals for a synergistic effect or worn by itself.

**Hematite** should be worn in a ring on the right hand. Hematite was often combined with turqoise for jewelry by Pueblo Indians.

**Jade** should be worn in combination with pearls.

**Jasper** should be worn just below the throat chakra. When combined with opal jasper heightens the effect of opals.

**Lapis lazuli** should not be placed directly on the body. According to Edgar Cayce, Lapis lazuli should be encased in thin glass if incorporated into jewelry.

**Malachite** should be worn about the neck.

**Opal** should be worn as a hat pin or over the crown chakra.

**Pearl** should be worn directly against the body.

**Peridot** should be set in gold to enhance its power.

**Rhodochrosite** should be set in pink gold to amplify its energy.

**Rose Quartz** should be worn against the chest.

**Ruby** should be worn on the left side of the body or on the center of the forehead.

**Sapphire** should be set in silver and worn as a ring on either hand.

**Sardonyx** should be worn as pins, buttons or amulets.

**Silver** should be worn alone or as a setting for stones in the blue, yellow and purple color ranges.

**Turquoise** should be set in silver and worn as a ring on the left hand or worn as a pendant about the neck.

# Meditating with Stones

Crystals have held a never ending fascination with people throughout millenium. Gazing upon a crystal has encouraged individuals to see the simple building blocks that make up our seemingly complex world. Holding a crystal in hand has calmed individuals, enabling them to listen to their inner self. Surrounding themselves with crystal points has given individuals the experience of feeling the energy these crystals impart. Peering into a crystal sphere has allowed individuals a view of their finer self. Below are a few of the ways individuals have used crystals to explore their world.

**Double Terminated Quartz Crystals**
1. While either lying down or sitting comfortably, hold a double terminated quartz crystal in each hand. Breathe deeply. Relax by envisioning a calm environment. Enjoy the peace for at least 5 minutes.

2. While lying down place a double terminated quartz crystal on the Third Eye, i.e., at the center of your forehead in line with your eyebrows. Or, while sitting, place a crystal on the Crown Chakra, i.e., the top of your head. Meditating with a double terminated quartz crystal is said to expand consciousness. It is also said to blend the physical, spiritual and intuitive aspects of your being.

## Crystal Points Meditations

1. With your back to the North, sit comfortably on the floor. With the terminations towards the South, place the clear quartz points on the floor in the following order: in front of you, to your left side, to your right side. Meditating in this fashion is said to enhance your physical being.

2. With your back to the North, sit comfortably on the floor. With the terminations also towards the North, place the clear quartz points on the floor in the following order: behind you, to your left side, to your right side. Mediatating in this fashion is said to enhance your emotional being.

3. While sitting on the floor, place the clear quartz crystals around you in a pattern that feels comfortable to you. Hold a double terminated quartz crystal in each hand. Feel the vibrations of the single terminated crystals. Feel the energy flowing into and out of the double terminated crystals. Feel the energy for at least 5 minutes.

4. Sitting comfortably on the floor place a clear quartz point to the right and rear of you. Place another clear quartz point to the left and rear of you. Place the third clear quartz point centered in front of you. Make sure that each of the crystal terminations is pointing towards your body. You may hold an amethyst point, a smoky quartz point or a crystal sphere as a focus. When using an amethyst hold it in your left hand with its termination towards your arm. When using a smoky quartz point hold it in either or both hands. Point its termination towards your body. When using a crystal sphere hold it in both hands.

Amethyst is said to humble oneself, allowing the mind to be receptive to new knowledge.

Smoky Quartz is said to help ground people who are ambivalent allowing them to be more receptive.


## Flourite Octahedron

1. While holding the flourite octahedron in your hand or up to a light, gaze upon its form. Look at the color variations. Peer into the crystal to look for evidence of depth, evidence

24

of trauma. See how the crystal has healed to become a beauty in its simplicity.

2. Lie down. Place a flourite octahedron on the center of your forehead. Be sure one of the points is touching your hairline. Breathe deeply. Calm your mind. Meditating in this fashion is said to direct energy into the consciousness.

**Amethyst Guided Sleep**
To inspire sweet dreams it is recommended to employ an amethyst crystal. Place the crystal up to your forehead. Program it to keep your mind free from risk while in the sleep state. Sleep with the amethyst crystal under your pillow.

These are just a few of the ways that individuals have used crystals to enhance meditation. Each crystal has its own energy vibration. You can use these examples as a starting point to learn about the vibrations of your crystals. Listen to your crystals and listen to your heart.

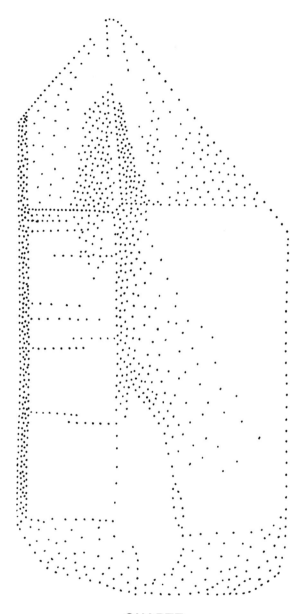

**QUARTZ**

26

# Numerical Vibration of Stones

According to Numerologists every name vibrates, moves, lives. Numbers are associated with each letter of the alphabet. And each number vibrates to a particular frequency. The number missing, due to the spelling of a name, indicates to the Numerologist what experience is needed in this lifetime to help complete the cycle of re-birth.

| 1 | 2 | 3 | 4 | 5 | 6 | 7 | 8 | 9 |
|---|---|---|---|---|---|---|---|---|
| A | B | C | D | E | F | G | H | I |
| J | K | L | M | N | O | P | Q | R |
| S | T | U | V | W | X | Y | Z |   |

Since particular frequencies draw certain experiences to you, the use of stones vibrating to that particular frequency may help in the cycle of re-birth. Following is a list of a stones and their vibratory numbers according to their names.

Stones vibrating to the number 1 (Independence):
    Almandine
    Aquamarine
    Azurite

Barite
Copper
Cowrie
Moss Agate
Obsidian
Pink Carnelian
Rock Crystal
Sunstone
Turquoise
Stone vibrating to the number 2 (Understanding for Others):
Gold
Stones vibrating to the number 3 (Creative Expression):
Amber
Amethyst
Azurmalachite
Chrysoprase
Lapis lazuli
Padparadschah Sapphire
Pyrite
Red Spinel
Ruby
Sardonyx
Schorl
Spinel
Sugilite
Stones vibrating to the number 4 (Work):
Black Sapphire
Bloodstone
Chiastolite
Emerald
Lazurite
Lead
Magnetite
Mercury
Moonstone
Pumice
Red Coral
Rhodochrosite
Rutile
Silver

Sodalite
Tiger Eye
White Sapphire
Zircon
Stones vibrating to the number 5 (Variety):
Alexandrite
Amazonite
Carnelian
Chrysocolla
Heliodor
Nephrite
Rubellite
Staurolite
Stones vibrating to the number 6 (Responsibility):
Blue Sapphire
Cat's Eye
Chrysoberyl
Citrine
Green Tourmaline
Jasper
Onyx
Peridot
Rutilated Quartz
Sard
Smoky Quartz
Star Sapphire
Topaz
Tortoise Shell
Stones vibrating to the number 7 (Bridging the Spiritual
and Material Worlds):
Aventurine Quartz
Blue Spinel
Flint
Flourite
Kunzite
Lazulite
Pearl
Platinum
Rose Quartz
Sulphur

Tin
Uvarovite
Stones vibrating to the number 8 (Material World):
Calcite
Celestite
Iris Agate
Ivory
Jet
Marcasite
Opal
Selenite
Serpentine
Stones vibrating to the number 9 (Universal Brotherhood):
Apatite
Chalcedony
Elbaite
Fire Agate
Hematite
Jadeite
Malachite
Pink Coral
Rhodonite
Tektite

## MASTER NUMBER STONES

Stones vibrating to the number 11:
Gypsum
Iron
Jade
Labrodorite
Meteorite
Sapphire
Snakeskin Agate
Watermelon Tourmaline
Stones vibrating to the number 33:
Black Coral
Diamond
Stone vibrating to the number 55:
Indicolite

# Mineral Families

To some people, one stone looks the same as another. That is why for many centuries all red stones were called ruby, all blue stones were called sapphire and all green stones were called jade. But with man's advancements in the field of Science, man was able to detect differences between stones of the same color. Man was able to determine varieties of crystal systems, the building blocks of minerals. Instead of a red stone being a ruby, it might be a garnet or a carnelian or a tourmaline, depending on its crystal habit.

Following is a list of numerous stones and the mineral families to which they belong. Within the brackets is the crystal system to which the family belongs. The illustrations may help you differentiate the crystal structure of the various families.

Most crystals are not perfect in regards to their crystal growth. Many crystals intergrow when forming to create *twins*. Twinning may involve more than two of the same crystal. *Sceptre* is another type of non-uniform crystal growth. When a crystal sceptres it noticably enlarges towards the top of the crystal. A delineation can be seen between the original crystal growth and later knob-like crystal growth. *Phantoms* are crystals that appear to have another of the same crystal inside of it. This can occur as

31

the crystal grows, that is, adds layer upon layer of minerals. For some reason there is a difference in two layers being laid down upon the crystal. This difference causes the appearance of a phantom within a crystal. Mineral *inclusions* also occur. Inclusions occur when crystals grow incorporating non-related minerals into the structure. Quartz crystals commonly include pyrite, rutile and tourmaline. This is because these minerals are often found forming in the same locations as quartz. Inclusions are considered beneficial and also help to create the rainbow patterns often seen within quartz crystals.

Beryl [hexagonal system]
    Aquamarine (blue)
    Emerald (green)
    Goshenite (clear)
    Heliodor (yellow)
Chrysoberyl [orthorhombic system]
    Alexandrite
    Cat's Eye
Corundum [hexagonal system]
    Leucosapphire (clear)
    Ruby (red)
    Sapphire (black, blue, yellow)
    Padparadschah (orange)
Feldspar [triclinic system]
    Amazonite
    Labrodorite
    Moonstone
    Sunstone
Garnet [cubic system]
    Almandine (red)
    Grossularite (greens)
    Melanite (black)
    Pyrope (brownish-purplish)
    Spessarite (orange colors)
    Uvarovite (emerald green)
Gypsum [monoclinic system]
    Selenite

Jade [monoclinic system]
    Jadeite
    Nephrite
Obsidian [amorphous system]
    Apache Tears
    Black
    Gold Sheen
    Mahogany
    Rainbow Sheen
    Silver Sheen
    Snowflake
Pyrite [cubic system]
    Marcasite
Quartz [hexagonal system]
    Rock Crystal (clear)
    Amethyst (purple)
    Citrine (yellow)
    Smoky (brown)
    Morion (blackish)
    Rose (pink, massive quartz)
    Rutilated (rutile in clear quartz)
    Prase (green, massive quartz)
    Tiger Eye (brownish-yellow asbestos replacement)
    Hawk's Eye (greyish-green asbestos replacement)
    Falcon's Eye (greyish-blue asbestos replacement)
    Silicified Wood ("petrified wood")
    Chalcedony (crypto-crystalline quartz)
        Agate, common
        Bloodstone
        Carnelian
        Chrysocolla
        Chrysoprase
        Flint
        Iris Agate
        Jasper
        Moss Agate (dendritic inclusions)
        Onyx
        Plume Agate (dendritic inclusions)
        Sard
            Sardonyx

Tourmaline [hexagonal system]
  Achroite (clear)
  Dravite (brown)
  Elbaite (pink)
  Green
  Indicolite (blue)
  Rubellite (red)
  Schorl (black)
  Siberite (purple)
  Watermelon (pink center, green rind)

There are six crystal systems, some of which were mentioned in the list above. The six systems are: *cubic* i.e. three crystal axes, all axes are of equal length, all axes intersect one another at 90° angles; *hexagonal* i.e. four crystal axes, three axes are of equal length and cross each other at 60° angles, the fourth axis is unequal and stands at right angles to the plane formed by the other three; *monoclinic* i.e. three crystal axes, all axes are of equal length, two axes intersect obliquely, the third axis intersects the other two at 90°; *orthorhombic* i.e. three crystal axes, all axes unequal in length, all axes at 90° angles to one another; *tetragonal* i.e. three crystal axes, all three axes intersect at 90° angles, two axes are of equal length, the third axis is unequal in length; *triclinic* i.e. three crystal axes, all axes are unequal in length, all axes intersect obliquely. Minerals also grow in a non-crystalline fashion referred to as *amorphous.*

# Bibliography

Baer, Randall N., and Vicki B. *Windows of Light.* New York: Harper & Row Publishers, Inc., 1984.

Ballard, Julliet Brooke. *Treasures from Earth's Storehouse.* Virginia Beach, Virginia: A.R.E. Press, 1980.

Bhattacharyya, Benoytosh. *Gem Therapy.* Calcutta, India: Firma KLM Private Limited, 1957.

Black, J. Anderson. *The Story of Jewelry.* New York: William Morrow and Company, Inc., 1973.

Bonewitz, Ra. *Cosmic Crystals.* Wellingborough, England: Turnstone Press Limited, 1983.

Borner, Rudolf. *Minerals, Rocks and Gemstones.* London: Oliver and Boyd, 1962.

Bryant, Page. *Crystals and Their Use.* Albuquerque, NM: Sun Publishing Co., 1984.

Burbitis, Philip W. *Quartz Crystals for Healing and Meditation.* Taylor, Arizona: The Universarium Foundation, Inc., 1985.

Buske, Terry. *Llewellyn's 1983 Moon Sign Book.* Saint Paul, Minnesota: Llewellyn Publications, 1982.

Cayce, Edgar. *Gems and Stones.* Virginia Beach, Virginia: A.R.E. Press, 1960.

Christian, Paul. *The History and Practice of Magic.* New York: The Citadel Press, 1963.

Crow, W.B. *Precious Stones: Their Occult Power and Hidden Significance.* Wellingborough, England: The Aquarian Press, 1968.

Deaver, Korra. *Rock Crystal: The Magic Stone.* York Beach, Maine: Samuel Weiser, Inc., 1985.

Evans, Joan. *Magical Jewels of the Middle Ages and the Renaissance.* New York: Dover Publications, Inc., 1976.

Fernie, William T. *The Occult and Curative Powers of Precious Stones.* New York: Harper & Row, Publishers, 1973.

Finch, Elizabeth. *The Psychic Value of Gemstones.* Jerome, AZ: Luminary Press, 1980.

Fisher, P.J. *The Science of Gems.* New York: Charles Scribner's Sons, 1966.

Glick, Joel, and Julia Lorusso. *Healing Stoned.* Albuquerque, NM: Brotherhood of Life, 1976.

Gregorietti, Guido. *Jewelry Through the Ages.* New York: Crescent Books, 1969.

Heiniger, Ernest A., and Jean. *The Great Book of Jewels.* Switzerland: Edita Lausanne, 1974.

Hodges, Doris M. *Healing Stones.* Perry, Iowa: Pyramid Publishers of Iowa, 1961.

Holroyd, Stuart. *Magic, Words, and Numbers.* London: Aldus Books Limited, 1975.

Hurlbut, Cornelius S. *Minerals and Man.* New York: Random House, 1970.

Isaacs, Thelma. *Gemstones, Crystals & Healing.* Black Mountain, N.C.: Lorien House, 1982.

Kunz, George Frederick. *The Curious Lore of Precious Stones.* New York: Dover Publications, Inc., 1947.

Kunz, George Frederick. *Planetary Influences and Therapeutic Uses of Precious Stones.* Santa Fe, NM: Sun Publishing Company, 1985.

Liddicoat, Richard T. *Handbook of Gem Identification.* Los Angeles, CA: Gemological Institute of America, 1951.

Littlefield, Charles, W. *Man, Minerals, and Masters.* Alburquerque, NM: Sun Publishing Company, 1937.

Powell, Neil. *Alchemy, the Ancient Science.* London: Aldus Books Limited, 1976.

Raphaell, Katrina. *Crystal Enlightenment.* New York: Aurora Press, 1985.

Richardson, Wally, and Jenny. *Spiritual Value of Gem Stones.* Marina del Rey, CA. DeVorss & Company, 1980.

Sinkankas, John. *Gemstones of North America.* New York: Van Nostrand Reinhold Company, 1959.

Smith, Michael G. *Crystal Power.* Saint Paul, Minnesota: Llewellyn Publications, 1985.

Soderstrom, Ruth. *Numerology: The Key to Spiritual Evolvement.* Tacoma, WA: The Metamorphosis Press, 1985.

Stewart, C. Nelson. *Gem-stones of the Seven Rays.* Adyar, India: The Theosophical Publishing House, 1939.

Uyldert, Mellie. *The Magic of Precious Stones.* Wellingborough, England: Turnstone Press Limited, 1981.

_____ *Gems, Stones, and Metals.* Heritage Publications, 1977.

Fisher, P.J. *The Science of Gems.* New York: Charles Scribner's Sons, 1966.

37

# Appendix

Stones of Aries (March 21 - April 19)
  Bloodstone
  Diamond
  Sard
  Zircon
Stones of Taurus (April 20 - May 20)
  Carnelian
  Emerald
  Selenite
Stones of Gemini (May 21 - June 20)
  Apatite
  Aquamarine
  Cat's Eye
  Celestite
  Chrysocolla
  Citrine
  Rutile
Stones of Cancer (June 21 - July 22)
  Moonstone
  Moss Agate
  Opal
  Pink Coral
  Serpentine

Stones of Leo (July 23 - August 22)
  Jasper
  Onyx
  Ruby
  Snakeskin Agate
  Sulphur
Stones of Virgo (August 23 - September 22)
  Amazonite
  Peridot
  Sapphire
Stones Of Libra (September 23 - October 22)
  Elbaite
  Nephrite
  Padparadschah Sapphire
  Sunstone
Stones of Scorpio (October 23 - November 21)
  Almandine
  Red Spinel
  Rubellite
  Watermelon Tourmaline
Stones of Sagittarius (November 22 - December 21)
  Azurite
  Labrodorite
  Lapis lazuli
  Sodalite
  Topaz
Stones of Capricorn (December 22 - January 19)
  Fire Agate
  Green Tourmaline
  Schorl
  Smoky Quartz
  Turquoise
Stones of Aquarius (January 20 - February 18)
  Rock Crystal
  Uvarovite
Stones of Pisces (February 19 to March 20)
  Amethyst
  Jade
  Sugilite

---

Stones of Pluto which rules Scorpio
  Alexandrite
  Flint
  Kunzite
  Rhodochrosite
Stones of Neptune which rules Pisces
  Cowrie
  Flourite
Stones of Uranus which rules Aquarius
  Aventurine Quartz
  Barite
Stones of Saturn which rules Capricorn
  Apache Tears Obsidian
  Black Coral
  Jet
  Lead
  Malachite
  Obsidian
  Tiger Eye
Stones of Jupiter which rules Sagittarius
  Blue Spinel
  Iris Agate
  Ivory
  Pumice
  Tin
Stones of Mars which rules Aries
  Hematite
  Iron
  Red Coral
  Sardonyx
Stones of the Sun which rules Leo
  Amber
  Chrysoberyl
  Gold
  Heliodor
  Pyrite
Stones of Venus which rules Taurus and Libra
  Chrysoprase
  Copper

Indicolite
Red Coral
Rose Quartz
Stones of Mercury which rules Gemini and Virgo
Lodestone
Mercury
Tortoise Shell
Stones of the Moon which rules Cancer
Calcite
Chalcedony
Iceland Spar
Pearl
Silver

———————————————————

Stones of the 1st Ray (Electric-blue; The Will)
Diamond
Magnetite
Rock Crystal
Zircon
Stones of the 2nd Ray (Indigo; Wisdom)
Lapis lazuli
Sapphire
Sodalite
Turquoise
Stones of the 3rd Ray (Green; Creative Activity)
Aquamarine
Emerald
Jade
Malachite
Peridot
Sardonyx
Stones of the 4th Ray (Orange; Rhythm/Harmony)
Chalcedony
Jasper
Serpentine
Snakeskin Agate
Tiger Eye
Watermelon Tourmaline

Stones of the 5th Ray (Yellow; Form/Stability)
  Amber
  Chrysoberyl
  Citrine
  Topaz
Stones of the 6th Ray (Crimson; Devotion)
  Almandine
  Carnelian
  Elbaite
  Green Tourmaline
  Red Coral
  Rhodonite
  Rubellite
  Ruby
Stones of the 7th Ray (Violet; Purpose)
  Amethyst
  Kunzite

— — — — — — — — — — — — — —

Stones of the 1st Chakra (Base of the Spine)
  Almandine
  Apache Tears Obsidian
  Bloodstone
  Fire Agate
  Onyx
  Rhodonite
  Smoky Quartz
Stones of the 2nd Chakra (Solar Plexus)
  Amber
  Carnelian
  Ruby
Stones of the 3rd Chakra (Spleen)
  Apatite
  Calcite
  Citrine
  Sulphur
  Topaz
Stones of the 4th Chakra (Heart)
  Chrysoprase

Elbaite
Emerald
Green Tourmaline
Kunzite
Malachite
Moonstone
Opal
Peridot
Rose Quartz
Sunstone
Watermelon Tourmaline
Stones of the 5th Chakra (Throat)
Amazonite
Aquamarine
Azurmalachite
Celestite
Chrysocolla
Turquoise
Stones of the 6th Chakra (Brow/Third Eye)
Amethyst
Azurite
Flourite
Labrodorite
Lapis lazuli
Sapphire
Sodalite
Sugilite
Stones of the 7th Chakra (Crown)
Alexandrite
Heliodor
Rock Crystal
Selenite

-------------------------

Stone of January
Garnet
Stone of February
Amethyst

Stones of March
  Aquamarine
  Bloodstone
Stones of April
  Diamond
  White Sapphire
  Zircon
Stone of May
  Emerald
Stones of June
  Alexandrite
  Moonstone
  Pearl
Stone of July
  Ruby
Stones of August
  Peridot
  Sardonyx
Stone of September
  Blue Sapphire
Stones of October
  Opal
  Tourmaline
Stone of November
  Topaz
Stones of December
  Lapis lazuli
  Turquoise

# Referral

Abundance—Green Tourmaline
Acceptance—Rhodochrosite
Accomplishments—Platinum
Achievement—Rhodonite
Activity—Pink Coral, Snakeskin Agate
Adaptability—Chrysoprase
Adrenal Glands—Chrysoberyl
Advantage—Silver
Agreement—Moss Agate
Allergies—Zircon
Amplification—Opal, Ruby
Anger—Chrysocolla, Peridot
Animation—Platinum
Anus—Smoky Quartz
Anxiety—Azurmalachite, Rhodonite
Art—Cowrie, Rose Quartz
Arthritis—Copper
Artistry—Cowrie
Aspiration—Fire Agate
Assimilation—Rhodochrosite
Asthma—Malachite
Astral Projection—Double Terminated Quartz Crystal,
    Magnetite
Attention—Pearl, Sapphire, White Sapphire

Attraction—Sugilite
Attunement—Jade, Red Coral
Aura—Labrodorite, Rutile
Aura Balancing—Labrodorite
Avoidance—Rhodochrosite
Awakening—Apatite, Iris Agate
Awareness—Selenite, Tiger Eye

Balance—Rutile
Beauty—Rose Quartz, Sapphire, Turquoise, Watermelon
    Tourmaline
Birth—Cowrie
Bladder Trouble—Jade
Blood—Iron
Blood Circulation—Chiastolite, Citrine, Copper
Body—Blue Sapphire, Hematite, Silver, Sugilite
Bone Marrow—Onyx
Bowel Cramps—Cat's Eye
Bronchitis—Pyrite, Rutile
Business—Amethyst, Citrine

Calming—Amethyst, Azurmalachite, Blue Spinel, Gold,
    Lazulite
Centering—Star Sapphire
Challenge—Smoky Quartz
Change—Obsidian
Charity—Chalcedony, Pearl
Cheerfulness—Lapis lazuli, Padparadschah Sapphire,
    Snakeskin Agate
Chest—Tin
Circulation of the Blood—Citrine, Copper
Clarity—Selenite
Cleansing—Silver
Coherence—Rhodonite
Colic—Red Coral
Comfort—Azurmalachite
Concentration—Flourite, Pearl, Ruby
Consciousness—Heliodor
Confidence—Azurite, Lapis lazuli, Opal, Topaz

Confusion—Apatite, White Sapphire
Constipation—Green Tourmaline, Platinum
Consumption—Tin
Continuity—Pink Coral
Controversy—Ruby
Cowardice—Diamond
Creativity—Bloodstone, Cowrie, Green Tourmaline, Red
    Coral, Rose Quartz, Sunstone, Topaz
Crops—Moss Agate

Danger—Fire Agate
Death—Jade
Decisions—Bloodstone, Onyx, Topaz
Demeanor—Citrine, Lapis lazuli, Padparadschah Sapphire,
    Snakeskin Agate
Denial—Rhodochrosite
Depression—Lapis lazul, Pumice
Desire—Blue Spinel
Despair—Pumice
Devotion—Rubellite
Digestion—Pearl
Direction—Rubellite
Dis-ease—Azurmalachite, Sugilite
Disputes—Ruby
Double Meanings—Iceland Spar
Dreams—Jade, Jadeite

Education—Citrine
Ego—Moss Agate, Peridot
Eloquence—Mercury
Emotions—Azurmalachite, Elbaite, Emerald, Hematite, Iron,
    Jadeite, Kunzite, Tektite, Watermelon Tourmaline
Emphysema—Rhodonite
Enemy—Flint
Energy—Calcite, Chalcedony, Elbaite, Hematite, Kunzite,
    Labrodorite, Platinum, Ruby, Rutile, Spinel
Enthusiasm—Elbaite
Envy—Carnelian
Evil Eye—Chiastolite, Sapphire

Experience—Tektite, Watermelon Tourmaline
Eye Disease—Tiger Eye
Eyesight—Opal

Faith—Pearl
Falls—Elbaite
Family—Citrine, Pink Carnelian
Fear—Carnelian, Diamond, Fire Agate, Jet, Sard, Tourmaline
Fearless—Sard
Feelings—Elbaite, Gold
Feminine Discomfort—Chrysocolla
Fertility—Cowrie
Fever—Chiastolite, Ruby
Fidelity—Malachite
Flaws—Obsidian
Focus—White Sapphire
Forgiveness—Chrysoberyl
Form—Pink Coral
Friendliness—Padparadschah Sapphire
Friendship—Barite, Iris Agate, Malachite, Pyrite, Sardonyx

Generosity—Chrysoberyl
Gland Metabolism—Sodalite
Glands, Swollen—Aquamarine
Goiter—Amber
Good Cheer—Snakeskin Agate
Good Fortune—Gypsum, Moonstone, Onyx, Sardonyx
Good-will—Chalcedony, Fire Agate
Grief—Onyx
Growth of Crops—Moss Agate

Happiness—Gold, Iris Agate, Moonstone, Onyx, Sardonyx
Harmony—Barite, Indicolite
Headache—Turquoise
Healing—Amber, Blue Sapphire, Gold, Rutile, Sugilite, Tin
Health—Iris Agate, Ruby
Hearing Problems—Snakeskin Agate
Heart—Blue Sapphire
Heart Trouble—Almandine